1993

Dearest Mummy

Many Happy returns to you
and have a great birthday

Fondest Love

Jonny +
Louise
x

Bath

in old picture postcards

by
Maria Joyce, formerly Bath Reference Librarian
and
H. Mary Wills, formerly Senior Assistant, Bath Reference Library

European Library – Zaltbommel/Netherlands

To Bath Reference Library, 18 Queen Square, 1964-1990.

Acknowledgements:
The authors are grateful for permission to use 138 postcards from the photographs collection at Bath Reference Library (Community Leisure Department, County of Avon). No. 130 is from the authors' collection; No. 105 was kindly lent by Cynthia Turner, to whom thanks are due for helpful advice. We are also indebted to Stephen Bird, Ted Dolman, Trevor Fawcett, Reverend G. Holden, G.F. Laurence, Jill Lethbridge, Colin Maggs, Beryl Martin, Clive Quinnell and Kelvin Thomas for help and information.
Many thanks to our colleagues at Bath Reference Library, who allowed us access to the collections in the turbulent weeks before the library's move to new premises. Special thanks to Mrs. Edna Pashley whose typing skill transformed drafts into a tidy manuscript.

GB ISBN 90 288 4995 5 / CIP

© 1990 European Library – Zaltbommel/Netherlands

INTRODUCTION

The story of Bath begins with a spring: the spring of hot mineral water which bubbles through the earth here. Evidence shows pre-Roman use of the water, and the Romans built a religious and recreational resort round the hot spring. Celtic Sulis was equated with Roman Minerva, and a large temple dedicated to Sulis Minerva was built at Aquae Sulis. Near the temple was a bathing complex, enlarged and altered during five hundred years of Roman rule.

From Roman times until the 20th century there has been a constant battle against mud from the spring and floods from the river. This has of course affected the town's development. The Roman baths were lost under silt, and a Saxon priory and subsequent small medieval town rose over the Roman ruins. It occupied a roughly circular area inside a loop of the Avon, above flood level, but still affected by the water from the hot springs. The City of Bath remained within its walls till the early 1600s, except for some buildings outside the North Gate, but was surrounded by small villages not far away.

In the 16th century the status of Bath changed: a Priory served by a small secular settlement became a City with a Charter. The baths were primitive but attracted notable visitors. By the 1690s, after James II's queen had conceived a son and attributed her success to the power of Bath's water, the City was about to expand.

John Wood the Elder (1704-1754), Ralph Allen (1693-1764) and Richard 'Beau' Nash (1674-1761) created a new city. Nash brought orderly behaviour, attracting visitors of all classes to gamble, take the waters and socialize. Allen quarried stone and made money. Wood brought a vision, based on a false premise, of Bath as a classical city, and persuaded wealthy men to invest in his architectural innovations, using Allen's stone. The 18th century saw the city expand north, south and west, outside the old walls. Expansion east was delayed until the Bathwick estates became available for speculative building. This was halted by Baldwin's bankruptcy, but continued in the next century.

The Victorian era began early in Bath: the Royal Victoria Park opened in 1830, and from then onwards the City Council, religious authorities and private citizens built, enlarged and rebuilt not only in the old city but in the surrounding parishes. Nationally-known architects like Sir Gilbert Scott, and local men like Goodridge, Manners, Wilson and Davis, designed villas, churches, schools and hotels. Building in the 20th century includes places of entertainment, houses (and flats), shops and civil engineering works. There have been few notable designs and some disastrous ones. Yet in spite of the bombs of 1942 and the official vandalism of the 1960s and 1970s, much remains from earlier centuries: the old city, Georgian Walcot and Bathwick, and later developments around the centre. The old independent parishes – like Widcombe, Twerton, Weston – are now part of the City. Other villages remain proudly outside, but their names link them to it – Batheaston, Bathampton and Bathford.

Our choice of illustrations was determined by the availability of postcards relating to these areas before the Second World War in the Library's collection, and the fact that we tried to avoid using cards which had already been reproduced in earlier publications of Bath views.

A book like this is possible only because of the craze for collecting postcards in the late 19th and early 20th century. There were clubs and journals to encourage collectors to buy and send yet more cards, and to keep them in touch with each other. Postcard publishers launched competitions and awarded prizes to those who had the largest collection of their respective postcards. This was a giant industry with an amazing inventiveness. Germany was at its centre. Here you could even find a postman selling picture postcards and stamps in public places and restaurants. The eager collectors could post their cards on the spot: the postman had a mailing box strapped to his back!

Britain joined the collecting mania later than countries on the continent. The opposition to postcards was strong: lack of privacy in this 'open communication' was deplored; it was also feared that the new form of correspondence was signalling the end of letter-writing as it used to be. With hindsight one can say that the change would have come anyway, but the postcard hastened it.

The Post Office Act of 1870 finally authorized the use of postcards, and the first ones – official and plain – were for sale on 1st October 1870. Privately printed postcards were only available from September 1894. Now the market was open for picture postcards. There were specifications ruling the size – minimum not less than 3½ by 2¼ inches – and the material – cardboard of the same thickness as for official postcards. Soon the British Post Office had to deal with an enormous increase in trade. In 1871 75 million postcards went through the post, 860 million were sent in 1908/9! Postage in 1910 for a card was a halfpenny, whilst it was one penny for a letter. Private telephones were not widely used then, but postal collections and deliveries were frequent and reliable. It was quite safe when expecting an urgent message, to say 'drop me a postcard', where today it would be 'give me a ring'.

The postcards reproduced here are arranged as follows: panoramic views 1 - 2; city gates and historical pageant 3 - 15; then topographically: old centre 16 - 49; northern old centre 50 - 54; outer centre 55 - 70; Bathwick 71 - 85; Lyncombe and Widcombe 86 - 94; Combe Down and Prior Park 95 - 101; Twerton 102 - 107; Weston 108 - 112; Victoria Park 113 - 116; Lansdown 117 - 129; Batheaston 130 - 131; Bathampton 132 - 137; Bathford 138-140.

Maria Joyce
H. Mary Wills

BATH.

Many Thanks for Owls
Jan 5th 1901
Mother

1. This unusual moonlit version of the most famous panoramic view of Bath, from Beechen Cliff, south of the River Avon, must have been taken before 1900, as the Empire Hotel was built 1900/01 and is not shown on this photo. Notable features of the city which are visible include the Abbey, of course, with a flag flying from its tower, St. James Church, with the tower showing clearly just below the Abbey, and the spire of St. John's Roman Catholic Church on the extreme right. The long row centre left is James Street West. Through the lower part of the picture runs the Great Western Railway, alongside is the river, with a crane working on the quayside. Across the river is the Old Bridge, with the Full Moon Hotel at the other end on the right. The message is intriguing: were the owls a Christmas present?

A PEEP FROM BEECHEN CLIFF-BATH

2. The crenellations along the bottom of this photo belong to the parapet of the railway arch over the main road just south of the Old Bridge. The large building just across the bridge is the newly-built (1933) Electricity Department showrooms. The Full Moon Hotel had stood on that site from 1831 until 1931. Further up Southgate Street is the church of St. James, where Littlewoods now stands, and very prominently alongside the great Abbey is C.E. Davis's Empire Hotel. Unfortunately no photograph can entirely do justice to the view from Beechen Cliff, and this one shows one of the hazards of trying to see Bath from this viewpoint: the trees from which Beechen Cliff derives its name.

THE NORTH GATE OF BATH. ABOUT 1650.

3. This set of four cards showing Bath's city gates is based on 1879 lithographs by William Lewis, who copied the details from 16th and 17th century maps, adding artistic embellishments such as people and trees. The North Gate was demolished as late as 1755, and stood alongside Upper Borough Walls, near what is now Habitat's corner. Through this gate, with its central arch ten feet wide and fifteen feet high, came the travellers from London and the north. In the niche above the arch was a statue: some say it represented Edward VI, but more likely it was Bladud, the mythical founder of Bath. Beside the gate was the church of St. Mary-by-Northgate, the nave of which was used as King Edward VI's Grammar School from about 1583 until the 1750s. Part of the church was also used as a gaol for many years – the inmates may have taught the schoolboys one or two extra curricular lessons!

THE EAST GATE OF BATH. ABOUT 1650.

4. East Gate is the smallest, least elaborate of the four, but it does have one advantage over the others: it is still standing, and can be seen behind the Guildhall, in Boatstall Lane. The East Gate was used to reach the river and the mill by the weir, and also served as a kind of 'back door' for local residents. It was left open at night when the bigger gates were locked, and late-comers could enter the city after dark at this little arch.

THE SOUTH GATE OF BATH. ABOUT 1650.

5. As the traveller came down towards Bath from the south, once the Old Bridge had been crossed, this South Gate would be the way into the city. It was a very imposing entrance, eleven feet wide and fifteen feet high, with four gables and the statues of Edward III, Bishop Ralph of Shrewsbury and Prior John de Walcote looking down on the visitor approaching the gate. The church beside the South Gate was St. James, first built on this site in the late 13th century, and replaced in 1768. The air raids of April 1942 left it a ruin, and it was finally demolished in 1957. The South Gate itself was knocked down in 1755 to widen the road into the city.

THE WEST GATE OF BATH. ABOUT 1650.

6. It looks more like a church than a gate, but the West Gate fulfilled an important function for many years as the best lodgings in Bath. It had been rebuilt in 1572 in preparation for Queen Elizabeth I's visit, and was enlarged in the next centuries to accommodate royal visitors who came to bathe in the waters. It was eventually demolished in 1776, but its name lingers on in Westgate Street, and Westgate Buildings.

Sack of Bath by the Saxons A.D. 577

7. This dramatic and completely fictional representation of the end of Roman Aquae Sulis A.D. 577 is a postcard from a set of eight by the official photographers − Lewis Bros. − for the Bath Historical Pageant, 1909. In December 1908 a public meeting decided to stage a Pageant in Bath, following the success of similar events in other places. Circulars asking for subscriptions were quickly sent out, and a Ladies Meeting in January 1909 took on the task of organising costumes, dancing and other feminine activities. Writers and composers were commissioned, actors, singers, musicians, hundreds of bit-players and seamstresses volunteered − not to mention horses (and pigs). By 17th July they were all ready for a press rehearsal, with journalists from Canada and USA, as well as Britain, to put out preliminary reviews. From 19th to 24th July the whole city was consumed with Pageant fever.

BATH HISTORICAL PAGEANT. 1909.
EPISODE III.
THE CROWNING OF KING EDGAR.

8. When Archbishop Dunstan crowned Edgar (the Peaceable) King of All England on Whit Sunday A.D. 973, in the 16th year of his reign, it was in the Saxon church at Bath, and certainly not a bit like this. With a cast of eleven speaking parts and 405 extras this was one of the more modest scenes in the Bath Pageant, performed in the open air in the Royal Victoria Park each day during the Pageant Week. Every one of the players, from the King down to the slaves, had to be dressed appropriately, and thoroughly rehearsed: it must have been a producer's nightmare.

The Bath Historical Pageant, 1909.

Episode V. Queen Elizabeth watching the Revels.

Lewis Bros.
Official Photographers.

9. Episode 5 of the Pageant was set in 1590 when Queen Elizabeth I granted the City Charter to Bath Corporation. She did not actually visit Bath in that year, so this is another fictional event created especially for the Pageant. The Queen visited Bath only once, in August 1574, although another trip was planned for 1602, but she died before it took place. The 1590 Charter confirmed the previous 12 Charters, from 1189 to 1552, and Bath measures its independent status from that date.

BLADUD & PIGS.

Lewis Bros.,Official Photo.

10. One of the Revels watched by Queen Elizabeth in Episode 5 was 'A Masque of Prince Bladud', telling the legend of Bladud, son of King Lud Hudibras, who contracted leprosy and was banished from court. He became a swineherd, and, naturally, the pigs became leprous too, but were cured after wallowing in a certain muddy pool. Pigman Bladud followed their example, was likewise cured, and subsequently restored to his father's side. The City of Bath was founded around the muddy pool and the medicinal waters were revered from then onwards. In the Pageant's list of performers the names of the pigs are not given, but, as this photo shows, real animals must have been used.

Battle of Lansdown A.D. 1643

11. Another artistic impression of the Bath Pageant shows the mortal wounding of Sir Bevil Grenville (or Granville) at the Battle of Lansdown, 6th July 1643. This was one of the many skirmishes of the Civil War. The City of Bath managed to remain on more or less good terms with both Royalists and Parliamentarians during this period, although it was Royalist-held. The battle on Lansdown Hill between Waller's Parliamentary force and Hopton's Cavaliers resulted in a win for the King's men, but was achieved with the loss of many on both sides, in particular Sir Bevil Grenville, commander of the Cornish pikemen, who received a blow on the head after his horse fell, and died from the injury. This action-packed picture, with screaming horse, startled drummer and Sir Bevil's feathered hat whirling to the ground is probably much more exciting than the amateurs' performances in Bath's Royal Victoria Park in 1909.

Glorious Time of Beau Nash A.D. 1752.

12. Richard Nash, Welshman, gambler and fortune-hunter, arrived in Bath in 1704, and found a squalid little provincial town, with bad lodging-houses charging extortionate prices for abysmal facilities. He made money at cards, made friends with the Master of Ceremonies, and succeeded him when he was killed in a duel. At once, in his white tricorn hat, and with the force of his personality, Nash began to bring order and refinement to the social scene. His first act as 'King of Bath' was to ban swords − a wise move, after the fate of his predecessor. By the time he died in 1761 at 87, Bath was transformed into a beautiful, well-ordered resort for all, from royalty downward. He made a fortune from his cut of the takings at the tables, and generously supported improvements in the city − music, theatre, hospital, assembly rooms, pump room − all benefitted from his money and influence, as well as countless other charities. He died almost penniless, but left Bath as a legacy to all.

Reception of Queen Charlotte in the Pump Room, Bath A.D. 1817.

13. This drawing of the episode in the Pageant shows the elderly Queen Charlotte surrounded by her ladies and courtiers meeting the Mayor of Bath. George III's much-loved consort arrived at Bath on 3rd November 1817 and stayed at 93 Sydney Place. She intended to remain for some time but the visit was cut short by the tragic death of the Prince Regent's only daughter during childbirth. News of Princess Charlotte's death reached the Queen at a banquet in Bath's Guildhall, and the distraught grandmother left at once for London. After the funeral she came back for a quiet month, taking the waters and recovering from the shock. It was the death of this princess which forced the Prince of Wales' brothers to marry to ensure the succession. The only child born as a result of these marriages was the future Queen Victoria, daughter of the Duke of Kent.

BATH HISTORICAL PAGEANT, 1909.
GRAND FINALE.

14. Each day's performance ended with a great March Past of the 3,000 players; but before the grand finale there was a scene depicting famous writers and their creations with Bath connections: Chaucer and the Wife of Bath, Shakespeare and his Sonnets (!), Sheridan, Jane Austen, Fielding with Tom Jones, and Dickens with Pickwick. Then after the literary people came a pretty piece of public relations: a tableau of young ladies representing towns named Bath in Canada and USA, sent by their home states and entertained by local hosts, in return for a lot of publicity. The Master of the Pageant was Frank Lascelles, writer, painter, sculptor, but best known just for organising Pageants. He had been made a Chief of the Iroquois Indians after the Quebec celebrations in 1908, and was to become a Chief of the Basutos in 1910 after his South African triumph. The final reward of the Bath Pageant was that there was enough money left over to repay the original subscribers.

15. Sir Donald MacLean, a Liberal, was M.P. for Bath from 1906-1910. His family came from the Outer Hebrides, but he himself practised as a solicitor in Cardiff when he was returned at the 1906 election with 4,102 votes. At Bath he held a series of open air meetings and lectured at the Literary and Scientific Institute on 'The House of Commons from within'. He would have also made his appearances at special local events, e.g. the closing day of the Pageant in 1909, the memorial service for the late King Edward at the Abbey, and the visit of the British Medical Association to Bath in 1910. Later in his political career, he was for a time leader of the Parliamentary Party. He resigned this post on Asquith's return to the Commons in 1922. This postcard was sent by MacLean on 29th December 1909 to a gentleman in Weston-super-Mare: a proud father announcing that 'Baby's name is Ian'.

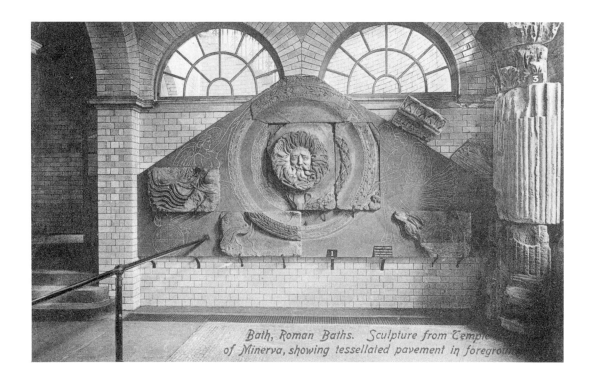

Bath, Roman Baths. Sculpture from Temple of Minerva, showing tessellated pavement in foreground

16. This view of the pediment over the entrance to the Temple of Sulis Minerva shows a reconstruction, incorporating the pieces discovered in 1790 while Thomas Baldwin was digging foundations for the new Pump Room. The Gorgon's head in the centre shows (unusually) a male Gorgon, with curling beard and moustaches, and hair comprised of snakes and wings. In one face the Celtic god Sulis was combined with the Roman goddess Minerva to express the linked attributes of both deities for this Roman British holy place. The tessellated pavement, described in the caption but almost totally obscured by the same caption, was discovered in 1897 when the Weymouth House School in nearby Abbeygate Street was being rebuilt. These two relics are no longer visible together, but have been placed in more appropriate parts of the modern Roman Baths Museum.

ROMAN BATHS OF BATH

AN EARLY BATH, LATER FILLED IN
FOR HYPOCAUSTS OF WHICH THE PILAE
CAN BE SEEN IN THE BACKGROUND.

17. The eastern end of the Roman baths complex, when it was built in the 1st century A.D., included this small plunge bath. The wall crossing the front left of this picture was part of a culvert, put in to carry water away when the bath itself was filled with rubble to form the base of a later suite of heated baths. The hypocaust, of which the remains can be seen in the background, provided the heat for the new baths. This area was first excavated in 1755, but the earliest level was not discovered until 1923.

ROMAN CULVERT FROM THE HOT SPRINGS AND SOUTH SIDE OF BATHS

THE GREAT CULVERT BUILT BY THE ROMANS FOR CARRYING OFF THE WASTE WATERS FROM THE BATHS IS STILL USED FOR ITS ORIGINAL PURPOSE.

ROMAN BATHS, BATH.

18. The drainage system installed by the Romans was very practical, with massive masonry built to withstand the force of constantly flowing hot water. Some of the places where smaller drains joined the main channel were equipped with access points from the surface above, so that workmen could get in to clear out silt and accumulated rubbish. Different levels were necessary, to lead the hot water from the spring to the Great Bath and on through the various parts of the bathing complex. This photo shows the steamy main drain which takes water away from the bath. The drain was discovered in October 1865 by J.T. Irvine, who was clerk of works for Sir George Gilbert Scott's restoration of Bath Abbey. He stayed twelve years in Bath, and made meticulous notes about the archaeological remains found under the old White Hart Hotel, and other Roman sites during those years.

19. Until almost the end of the 19th century most of the Roman remains in Bath still lay undiscovered. In the 1870s Bath Corporation were able to buy property near the known area of the Roman baths, and excavations were carried out over a period of several years, under the direction of Major C.E. Davis, the City Architect. This photo shows what was being discovered about 1888 beneath the former Bath Poor Law Union offices at 5 Abbey Street. On the left are Roman pillars and odd pieces of carved stone. At the centre can be seen a massive chunk of the vaulted box-tile roof, lying where it had fallen in the bottom of the Great Bath. On the floor some of the enormous lead sheets are also exposed to the open air. The steps at the right lead down into the eastern end of the bath, and on towards further discoveries. Meanwhile, the Kingston Billiards Rooms in the background were still going about their business.

20. Although the bases of the pillars are Roman, the covered colonnade was only built in 1897, and is nothing like the original appearance of the Great Bath. The heap in the foreground is a collection of Roman box-tiles, of which a great many have been discovered during excavations. Box-tiles were used for different purposes: some carried heated air under the floors, or up inside the walls, to create the hot dry atmosphere for the sauna-like caldarium, and others were used in the roof, being obviously lighter in weight than solid tiles.

Roman Bath and Abbey View, Bath   'Westfield' 277

21. Through the arches can be seen the archaeological diggings in progress in 1923 on the site of the old Kingston Baths. When they were being built in 1755 Roman remains were discovered, but were reburied until 175 years later when this east end of the Great Bath was again accessible. Luckily the lower layers were largely undamaged by the 18th century foundations. The 'Roman' figures looking down into the bath were put there in 1897.

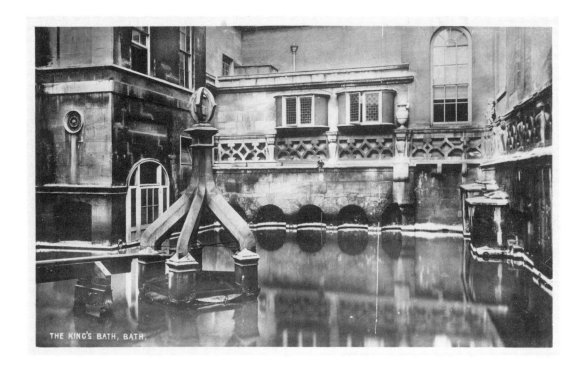

THE KING'S BATH, BATH.

22. The Roman baths disappeared under a layer of mud and were lost until 1755, but the springs continued to provide hot water. By at least the 13th century there was a public bath over the spring, owned by the Crown and called the King's Bath. In the open air men and women would soak for an hour or more, sometimes standing under the arches, holding brass rings set in the walls. Until the early 17th century they bathed naked. This scandalous situation was much criticised, and eventually linen shifts or drawers had to be worn. In the centre was the conduit decorated with (from 1664) an elaborate cross shaped cover. The one shown here was installed around 1880 and in 1979 this was removed, and has not been replaced. Around the bath is the elegant balustrade provided by Francis Stonar in 1697. The white line around the bath shows where the walls below water level were regularly whitened for cleanliness.

BATH. TERRACE OVERLOOKING THE ROMAN BATH.

23. The impressive toga-clad statues looking down on the Roman bath below appear to have been there for centuries, but are late Victorian. This view is taken from the terrace in the Pump Room extension which was designed by John Brydon and opened in 1897 by the Duke of Cambridge. The whole scheme cost £30,000, and included drawing and smoking rooms, and a concert room as well as the Roman Promenade around the Great Bath, and the terrace pictured here. Because there was too much fresh air in the winter on the terrace, a removeable glazed framework was fitted in 1904, and taken out each summer. This photo, with the dying tulips inside and the window space open, was probably taken about early June in the 1930s.

24. This sedan, or glass chair, appears to have been parked in the Roman baths to enable a sufferer to bathe: but it is more likely placed here merely to give the photographer enough daylight for his picture. The earliest enclosed chairs for carrying invalids in Bath from the 1630s were simple covered frameworks, with a low seat, a curtain at the front and short poles for the chairmen. The glass chair proper, with windows, a hinged front door and later a domed roof and other refinements, reached Bath at the end of the 17th century. It created employment for the strong men of the city, caused congestion, and obstructed pedestrians either when parked or travelling at running speed. The City formulated rules, set the rate of charges, and issued licences to the chairmen, who would in turn act as special constables, or cause their own riots, depending on their mood. Chairmen and chairs disappeared in the 1850s, after 150 years of service in Bath.

The Pump Room, Bath.

25. Overlooking everything is the giant electrolier, put up when electricity was installed in the late 1890s. This art nouveau extravaganza, once likened to 'a set of instruments for an American band', was removed for safety at the start of the Second World War. Afterwards a chandelier from the Assembly Rooms hung here until 1959, when a reproduction 18th century cut-glass one was made in Spain. At the far end of the room stands the oak-cased timepiece which Thomas Tompion made and gave to Bath in 1709, in gratitude for being cured by the waters, but maybe also as an advertisement in such a prestigious location. Above the clock is Prince Hoare's 1751 sculpture of Beau Nash which, like the clock, was originally placed in the 18th century Pump Room. It is strangely fitting that Nash should here preside over a Pump Room he would not recognise, but which was built to accommodate the greater numbers of visitors drawn to the city as a result of his activities.

BATH. THE CONCERT ROOM, ROMAN PROMENADE.

26. This splendid concert room for high class concerts was one of the additions to the Pump Room complex built in 1897 by John Brydon. Bath has had a long history of excellent music. In the 18th century Beau Nash hired a special band or orchestra to provide entertainment, and later Venanzio Rauzzini was responsible for organising regular concerts. In the 20th century the Bath Festival has continued the tradition, for many years under the direction of Yehudi Menuhin. However, the beautiful concert room has such atrocious accoustics that it is no longer used for its original purpose, and now merely acts as a vestibule for the main Pump Room.

27. The fountain stands like an altar, in front of stained glass windows, with solemn servers awaiting the faithful behind the rail. Every day a quarter of a million gallons of hot (46.5°C) mineral water pours out of the ground beneath their feet. This has attracted millions of people to Bath since pre-Roman times, although drinking the water was only introduced in the 17th century. Here are jugs lined up ready, filled with the healing water, memorably described by Sam Weller in Dickens' 'Pickwick Papers' as having 'a very strong flavour of warm flat irons'. The stained glass, of course, portrays scenes in Bath's history, from Bladud's pigs, through Roman soldiers, and King Edgar's coronation, to the visits of the Queens Elizabeth I and Anne. The statuette of the Angel at the Pool of Bethesda was presented in 1889 by the sculptor John Warrington Wood, and now stands at the entrance to the Pump Room.

BATH   MINERAL WATER FOUNTAIN IN THE PUMP ROOM

C4. King's and Queen's Baths. View of Stall Street entrance. c. 1890.

28. Several questions are posed in this 1890s photo: why is one of the men wearing a basket on his back? Who was the shadowy lady passing or standing between the posters? What was being performed at the Pump Room Concerts advertised on the posters? Some other oddities can be explained more easily: the large shadow across the right foreground is cast by Pieroni's mineral water fountain; the horizontal lines across the cobbled road are the rails laid here in 1880 for the city's horse trams; and the splendid conveyance (with attendants) parked on a basket-weave ramp in the doorway is a genuine bath chair, used to bring invalids to the King's and Queen's Baths, of which this is the west entrance. The ground floor pedimented storey was built in 1790/1 by Thomas Baldwin, and the upper storey, designed by C.E. Davis in 1886, was later removed, and replaced by a small glass dome as Baldwin had intended.

Bath, Mineral Water Fountain

29. Stefano Pieroni, a sculptor who lived at 4 Bath Street for many years, designed this fountain for the end of the street, to replace an earlier one. It gave the only free supply of Bath spa water: the other mineral water fountains were only for paying customers, at the Pump Room or in the baths. Originally the fountain had a large vase on top, and figures of the four seasons round the base. The vase was moved to Victoria Park, and a statue of Bladud put on the fountain. In the 1870s Bladud and the seasons were removed, and creepers covered the fountain. It was expensively restored in 1977 by Wessex Newspapers, but in the late 1980s the whole structure was moved to a new site in Terrace Walk. Now common tap water gushes behind a five foot railing, out of reach of the thirsty public. On the left of the card can be seen Goad's Bookshop, with Macdonald's Teeth Manufacturing Co., above. On the back the message reads: 'Dear Dad, shall be home in a few minutes. Alf.' What a postal service!

30. An undated view of the Grand Pump Room Hotel, which was built in 1869 on the site of an old coaching inn, the White Hart. The Corporation wanted to call the new luxury hotel 'Bath Forum House', and this was the title of the competition. Eleven architects submitted their plans, and finally William John Willcox and James Wilson's design was accepted. Both architects set up a company to raise the capital for building the hotel.

Grand Pump Room
Hotel, Bath. 137

31. This view of about 1912 shows the Pump Room Hotel in its heydays before the First World War. The management boasted that it was 'the only hotel in Bath with private lift and stairway direct to the Mineral Baths'; and there were 'radiators everywhere'. Visitors could announce their arrival by telegram using the official telegraph address: PUMPOTEL, Bath. The hotel was requisitioned by the Admiralty during the Second World War and used by them until 1942, when they moved to the Warminster Road hutments. The hotel remained empty and was demolished in 1958/9. Apparently the Civil Servants during their stay found it far from grand: the building was in a bad condition, with cracks in the outside walls. Countless cockroaches lived in the kitchen and cellars.

Inspection by Miss Baden Powell
of Girl Guides, at Bath N° 1

32. Miss Baden-Powell paid this visit to Bath on Saturday, 10th July 1916. The inspection of the local companies of Girl Guides took place in the Abbey Churchyard: the west door of the Abbey is in the background, the Rebecca fountain can be seen on the left. Agnes Baden-Powell (1858-1945) had founded the Girl Guides, together with her brother, in 1910. She was their National Vice-President and worked hard for the movement. Among her other interests were organ music, bee-keeping and bicycle-polo.

33. Another view of the Guides' rally, showing the business of J.R. D'Olier, surgeon chiropodist to the Royal Family at 9, Abbey Churchyard, and of George Louis Skrine, watchmaker and jeweller, at No. 10. Mrs. Paisey also traded at No. 9, she was an umbrella maker, and an umbrella shop used to be at this address until well into the 1970s. The programme for this day included lunch at Citizen House and, after the inspection, a meeting at the Pump Room. Here Miss Baden-Powell was presented by the St. Agnes Company with a travelling clock in a case, 'as a token of their esteem and love'.

ABBEY CHURCH YARD, BATH.

Ho356.

34. The view of the Abbey Church Yard in 1935 is typical of the pre-war atmosphere of the city, with the flower sellers guarding their paper-wrapped bouquets, and four bath chairs lined up waiting for clients. The few pedestrians hurry through a clean and tidy yard, past dark shops on the left – Mrs. Warwick's antiques, and the hairdresser above; next door the old Information Bureau and, further along, Paisey's the umbrella-makers. On the right looms the grimy north side of the Pump Room, with plain notices advertising the offerings within – 'Revels of 1935' – and further along is a high-handled bicycle (with a front basket) leaning trustfully against the railings.

35. Bath's Saxon church, where King Edgar was crowned in A.D. 973, and the later Norman cathedral have both disappeared. The present Bath Abbey was begun in the late 1490s by Bishop Oliver King, but was unfinished at the dissolution of the monasteries in the 1530s. When Queen Elizabeth I came to Bath in 1574 she was shocked by its ruined state, and ordered that it should be restored. Since then it has been rebuilt and altered, reflecting the growth of the city itself. Until 1833 the turrets on the tower were unembellished, but in that year pinnacles were added, also flying buttresses each side of the nave, and the turrets on this east front were changed from square to octagonal. The trees partly hiding the Abbey are in Orange Grove. In the foreground are the Parade Gardens, with the Angel of Peace, a memorial to Edward VII, which was moved to this site in 1934 from its original home at the top of Milsom Street.

BATH ABBEY FROM THE RIVER

Bath from the Empire Hotel

36. Soaring above the rest of this part of Bath is the spire of St. John's Roman Catholic Church. The church itself, designed by Charles Hanson, was built in 1863 and the spire added in 1867. Beyond the Institution Gardens is the imposing Georgian North Parade, built in 1740. Originally meant to be part of a greater scheme for the south of the city to match his development at Queen Square and the northern side of Bath, John Wood the Elder designed various decorative features for this block, but the owners refused to carry out his plan for such ornamentation. The unattached wing at the left is Duke Street, another part of Wood's grand design. The small church with a spire in the middle distance is St. Matthew's, Widcombe, with the Lyncombe valley behind it.

Bath- The Institution Gardens.

37. This pretty picture from a coloured original, shows the Institution Gardens in 1907, with trees in full leaf, red hollyhocks and other flowers and shrubs in the long borders, and the delicate bandstand. The Royal Literary and Scientific Institution had a large building, out of sight on the right of this view, which was opened in 1825. Until 1932 the Institution remained there, running lectures, a library, a museum and these grounds. In the foreground is the louvred wooden structure which housed their instruments for taking meteorological observations. The bandstand was replaced by an oak version in 1925, and the Institution building was demolished in 1932 to make way for a new road scheme.

38. Electric tram services in the city had only recently officially opened, when this photograph was taken from the roof of the Abbey. Tram No. 7 on the left is going out to Lambridge, No. 3 to Twerton. There was much other activity in the street on this busy working day − hopefully the dog reached the other side safely! In 1903 J.R. Goddard, commission agent and fruiterer, was trading at No. 14, next door to Dawson's, and Frederick Wright, cigar merchant, was advertising at 17, Northgate Street. The new wings of the Guildhall, designed by John McKean Brydon and built at a cost of £125,000, were completed in 1895.

39. Before the Empire Hotel opened its doors to visitors in 1901, a long and often embittered debate had taken place. It concerned the construction of a new road − from Orange Grove to Newmarket Row − and a building lease of the Boatstall Lane site, and land adjoining, for the purposes of erecting a grand hotel. The road was constructed, and the hotel was finally built by Major Davis. Its size and mixture of architectural styles have caused comments ever since. From 1939 to 1989, when the staff moved to new premises at Pinesway, the building was used as Ministry of Defence offices. There are now plans to make it into a hotel again. Pulteney Bridge, built by Robert Adam 1769-1774, is here seen with the old weir. In 1971 a new one was built as part of the River Authority's flood protection scheme.

DOCTOR OLIVER
INVENTOR OF THE
ORIGINAL BATH OLIVER BISCUIT

40. Thomas Hudson's portrait shows Dr. William Oliver in the 1740s. He came to Bath in 1728 as a physician to the sick and healthy taking the waters. Many suffered from obesity, and Oliver invented a plain biscuit, insisting his dyspeptic patients take them with water, instead of their usual rich diet. He made the biscuits in his kitchen, later passing the secret recipe to his ex-coachman John Atkins, who set up a bakery in Green Street. The business and the recipe have changed hands often, and the secret is now owned by the giant Nabisco Group. Oliver was a founder of the Mineral Water Hospital, and became one of its first physicians when it opened in 1742. He retired in 1761 and died at his Manor of Weston three years later.

Royal Mineral Water Hospital, Bath, Chapel.

41. Until 1861 patients at the Mineral Water Hospital were expected to attend either the Abbey or another designated place of worship regularly, and were allowed out especially to attend services. When the west wing extension was built, on the site of the old Abbey Rectory, the architects Manners and Gill included a chapel in their plans, so patients no longer needed to parade through the streets of Bath to attend church. The seven windows in the apse appropriately all show biblical scenes relating to water. The chapel was built to hold 150 people. In April 1942 the hospital extension, including the chapel with its beautiful windows and ceiling, organ, altar, pews and other furnishings, was badly damaged. As a result of a long campaign led by Dr. G. Kersley the extension was rebuilt, and opened again in 1965. The chapel itself was reconstructed, with new glass by Farrar Bell, depicting the same watery scenes of the original windows.

ABBEY GREEN. BATH.

42. Here is Abbey Green in about 1905. The buildings, varying from late 17th to early 19th century, were erected on what had once been part of the Abbey grounds, later a bowling green, but in this view only the tree would have been green. The London plane was planted about 1790, so it was just over a hundred years old when this photo was taken. Nowadays it is much fatter, and is surrounded by a grassy lawn. Evans Private Fish Bar has expanded into a large restaurant (built 1959), Marks & Spencer's 1973 archway links the two blocks shown here to make a more unified whole, and the other properties have been renovated to create a very attractive corner of Bath.

43. This imposing double-fronted house, No. 3 St. James Street South, was the last surviving example of William Killigrew's work, until it was demolished in 1959 to make way for Woolworth's new store (now Littlewoods). Killigrew, a joiner who became an architect, designed and erected several pre-Palladian buildings in the early 18th century before John Wood began to change the face of Bath. Among his other works were the Weymouth House School, the old Blue Coat School, and the south front of the Old Guildhall, all of which had disappeared by the time this building was knocked down. John Wood did not admire Killigrew, but it seems a pity that this particular example of his work has been replaced by a 1960s store.

44. Built by William Killigrew for Dr. Bellenson in 1720 on the site of an earlier house, this shows what remained of Weymouth House about 1920. Originally meant to be two small dwellings, they were made into one large house, and became the property of the Thynne family, one member of which, Viscount Weymouth, gave it the name by which it was known from the mid-18th century. In the 1790s it became the main city Post Office, but in 1816 much of it was demolished, and a circular building erected at the back for the Weymouth House Schools. In 1897 the circular building was demolished, and replaced by new school premises, leaving this part of the house for the caretaker's use. The motto on the corner 'Fear God and Honour the King', and its crown on a cushion appear to have been painted directly on the stone wall. In 1961 the whole of this building was demolished, and its site now lies under the back of Marks & Spencer's store.

45. Part of Chandos Buildings was leased in 1913 by Miss Helen Augusta Hope. She had been elected Bath's first woman Councillor in 1909, and devoted her life to the welfare of the citizens. As President of the local W.E.A. and vice-chairman of Bath Aid Co-ordination Committee she thought Bath needed a social and educational centre. She renamed No. 2 Chandos Buildings 'Citizen House', went to live there, and organised a library, reading room and classroom open to all every day. In the First World War she ran a canteen there for troops, and The Little Theatre began upstairs. After Miss Hope's death (1922) the centre became primarily a place for drama, with a collection of costumes and other relics. On 23rd February 1936 there was a serious fire which destroyed the beautiful staircase and much of the contents, along with the Employment Exchange next door. A second fire in 1944 finally destroyed the house.

Staircase. Citizen House. Bath. This fine house was built in 1727 for James Duke of Chandos. It formed part of a large three sided court, one of the first architectural designs of John Wood, Senior. It overlooked the city walls near the west gate, beyond which lay the Kingsmead and the open country. It is now used as a centre for social work.

46. Hetling Court was named after William Hetling, a successful wine merchant of the 18th century, who was in business at Hungerford House, also known as Hetling House, and now as the Abbey Church House. It can be seen on the left. When this picture looking towards Westgate Buildings was taken in 1922, John Hale had outlets for his business in antiques on either side of the Court, at No. 2 and No. 9. The fruit and potato stores advertised on the sun blinds belonged to W.H.C. Coles, who traded at 15, Westgate Buildings. His premises and the adjoining houses on the left have since gone, the buildings of the Technical College can now be seen from the photographer's viewpoint.

47. The Reverend Charles W. Shickle came to Bath from Norwich in 1865 as a young man to become curate at Twerton. After serving at Woolley and Langridge and teaching at Bath College, he became Master of St. John's Hospital. Here he stayed for 28 years, until his death in 1927. He was a gifted scholar, and he had spare time. He put this to good use by translating the ancient documents in Latin and Norman French in the possession of Bath Corporation, and transcribing other city documents. His transcripts of parish registers of Bath churches are a bonus to family researchers. Mr. Shickle had five daughters and died at the age of 86. The last of his daughters, Miss Gertrude Shickle, only died in 1972, aged 98. Friese Greene, the Bristol born pioneer of cinematography, took this portrait in Bath at his Gay Street studio between 1882 and 1888. He also had a studio at the Corridor from 1880 to 1888, and simultaneously maintained establishments in London and Brighton.

48. Trim Street was a new fashionable part of Bath just outside the city wall, when General Edward Wolfe (1685-1759) took a house for his family here. The first houses in the street were built in 1707. St. John's Gate, now Trim Bridge, was opened up for access when Queen Square was developed in 1728. No. 5 was built before that, around 1720, and because of its style has been attributed to Thomas Greenway, a Widcombe mason, who with his sons did reputable work carving vases and other architectural ornaments for new buildings in Bath. James Wolfe was born 1727 and entered the army at 14. He probably spent only short periods at his parent's house. As Major-General he led the British Army against the French to victory and fell at Quebec at the age of 32. The military emblems over the entrance of No. 5 were added later. The building now contains the offices of Stonechester Ltd. The shop next door was Frederick Brooks' bakery and confectionery in the 1930s, when this picture was taken.

49. This view taken in the 1930s shows the street on the other side of St. John's Gate on a rainy day. Building of houses in Queen Street also began in 1707. All the buildings are now Grade II listed, including St. John's Gatehouse spanning the street. Jill's Grill was at No. 3 from 1933 to 1955; the premises then became Queen's Restaurant and are now the Canary Café. The door straight ahead leads into R.J. Bossi's watch and clockmaker's business at 2, Trim Bridge, where the Trim Bridge Galleries are now.

Bath. Milsom Street.

50. Posted in 1906, this coloured card shows a very busy Milsom Street at the beginning of the century, with horse, cycle and foot traffic going both ways. At the top is the imposing front of Edgar Buildings, erected in 1761, before Milsom Street itself was built on Charles Milsom's garden (1762-1775). Originally a residential street, it soon became Bath's best shopping area, with silk mercers, glovers, tailors, goldsmiths, photographers, fine china shop, a ladies' club, and at least six banks, among others. J.R. Huntley's provision shop at No. 1 on the left was established in 1892/3, remaining there till the late 1940s. On the right behind the horse and carriage is the painted sign of H.H. Edmunds, court hairdresser, advertising manicures and face massages as well as beard trimming and other services.

51. Originally called Axford Buildings, this terrace was begun about 1769, and has been attributed to Thomas Farr Atwood — Bath plumber, builder, banker and Councillor — who also designed the adjoining Paragon. From the 1860s the two rows were numbered as one and 12 Axford Buildings became 33 Paragon. John Axford, after whom the terrace was named, had been a former landowner and Mayor of Bath and died in 1698. Sarah Siddons often stayed at No. 12/33 in the early 19th century: her husband William lived here permanently, and died in the house on 12th March 1808, one month after Sarah's last appearance on the Bath stage. She had made her name in Bath between 1778 and 1782 — probably lodging in Southgate Street — and often returned to perform at the Theatre Royal. Miss Ellen Terry unveiled a tablet on the wall on 17th October 1922: as a 16 year old she had played Titania at the Bath Theatre in March 1863 when it was re-opened after the disastrous fire.

52. On the left was the auctioneer A.C. Turpin, on the right is St. Michael's Church, and on the ground floor a bookshop, but the main building here is the Saracen's Head, originally medieval with early Georgian alterations. This was where Charles Dickens stayed in 1835, noting down local names, local characters and places which re-appeared in 'Pickwick Papers' (1836/7). This picture dates from about 1902, a year or two after Leonard Berman took over the Circulating Library and Bookshop from Richard Collard, although Collard's sign is still painted on the shop's side wall. To the left of the pub's entrance is a cycle store, which may belong to the Saracen's Head, but possibly was used by Fred Jelf, a cyclemaker who had premises nearby in 1901/2.

53. Tradition has it that Dr. Samuel Johnson lodged at the Pelican Inn with Boswell in April 1776, but evidence shows that Johnson actually stayed with his friends the Thrales at North Parade. Only Boswell, who was disliked by the Thrales, stayed at the Pelican. In the 1850s the name was changed to The Three Cups, and at sometime a malthouse was built over the garden. At the time of this photo about 1930 the Inn at 40 Walcot Street had deteriorated. In the late 1930s it became derelict and the business was transferred to 8 Walcot Street. The old Pelican was demolished in 1948, and this historic 17th century building was lost.

FARSON'S YARD, WALCOT ST. BATH

54. In the late 19th century Parson's Yard, with the slaughter houses (behind the photographer) built right down to the river, was the subject of reports to the Corporation's Sanitary Committee, because of its unsavoury condition. By the time this picture was taken about 1930 at least this dwelling had been made fairly pleasant for the woman shown here: whitened walls, flower pots and window boxes, a shrub in the corner and several washing lines. Through the opening on to Walcot Street can be seen the hairdressing premises of William Brown. Parson's Yard was three doors down from the old Pelican Inn, and was swept away at the same time as the Inn. The new Podium shopping centre, with Waitrose, the car park and the Hilton Hotel have completely obliterated this little corner of Bath.

North Parade Bridge,
Bath. 1004.

55. This placid scene shows a glimpse of Pulteney Bridge through the single span of North Parade Bridge in the early years of this century. By the end of the 18th century there were two bridges in the city: the Old Bridge and Pulteney Bridge. In one decade (1827-1836) two new iron bridges across the Avon were built as private ventures to link the burgeoning suburbs south and east of the river with the heart of the old city. First was Cleveland Bridge in 1827, then came this one, in 1835/6, designed by William Tierney Clark (who also designed London's Hammersmith Bridge). For 100 years its ironwork was on view, but in 1936 drastic alterations were made, and the remains of the iron bridge are now invisible, enclosed in stone.

La Sainte Union Convent, Bath.

M.J.R.B. 2526

56. Sisters of La Sainte Union came to Bath from Douai in France in 1858 at the invitation of the Benedictine Fathers to help with their educational programme. The convent at the junction of North Parade and Pulteney Road was built in 1861. The school was first a boys' boarding school, and later became a grammar school for girls. A separate prep school opened in Lyncombe Vale in 1953. When the convent closed down in 1979, the senior school merged with Cardinal Newman School at Odd Down to form St. Gregory's Comprehensive, and the girls over 16 continued their studies at St. Brendan's, Bristol, which was transformed into a Sixth Form College. The convent building was converted into offices for the probation service, and the new Magistrates' Courts were built on the site behind it.

57. When this photograph of the Forum was taken, the 1935 Gaumont film 'King of the Damned' was being shown there. Built by the architects W.H. Watkins from Bristol and E. Morgan Willmott from Cardiff, the Forum had opened its doors to the public in May 1934 with the film 'Evergreen' starring Jessie Matthews. It closed as a cinema in 1968, was then occasionally used for big orchestral concerts and regularly for bingo and films. There were plans to promote it as an arts centre, convert it into a shopping complex, a conference centre and concert hall. In 1988 Bath City Church bought it for use as their headquarters and meeting place for their members. As an exceptionally complete example of an art deco cinema, the Forum is included in the Department of the Environment's record of listed buildings and given Grade II.

58. Although he is called a fruiterer and florist, only a few apples hide among a mass of flowers in William H.A. Trimby's shop at 29 Charles Street in the 1920s. He bought the premises in 1919, and sold out to A.J. Caudle in 1928. Mr. Trimby moved to Saltford, but Caudle's flower shop is still flourishing.

59. When Mr. Trimby entered a display in the Bath Chrysanthemum Show at the Pump Room in November 1921 he chose to make a model of Blaise Castle, Bristol, and won a gold medal for it. Having electric light in the windows, installed by a nephew of J.A. Roebuck Rudge (inventor in the 1860s of the biophantascope, forerunner of cinematography), must have helped. Probably errand boy Raymond Trimby, on the right, helped too.

FIRST CHURCH OF CHRIST, SCIENTIST ~ BATH.

60. This imposing early Victorian building, with its classical Corinthian portico, near the Charlotte Street car park, was designed by James Wilson in 1845. It was built for the Moravians of Bath, to replace their 18th century chapel at nearby Princes Street, which was too small for 19th century needs. It has been said that the building was meant to be a copy of the Temple of Vesta at Tivoli, but in fact only the capitals of the columns were taken from that design. Wilson here designed not only a new church for the Moravians, but also a house each for the minister and the caretaker, and schoolrooms for adults and children, all for a cost of £2,700. In 1907 the Moravians decided to build a new base in a more residential part of Bath, and sold their city centre premises to the Christian Scientists.

61. When the church was built in 1845 it had seating for 300 people, although the number of attendants recorded at the 30th March 1851 census were, in the morning 390 and in the evening 200: it must have been extremely crowded in the morning! The Christian Scientists bought the church in 1907, and remained there until 1986, when they sold it for £200,000. Since then it has been renamed Queen Anne House, and has been adapted as a business training centre by New Work Trust.

FIRST CHURCH OF CHRIST, SCIENTIST - BATH.

62. Before the building of St. Andrew's was completed in 1873 (by Sir George Gilbert Scott), there was only one church, St. Swithin's, for the large parish of Walcot where baptisms and marriages could be solemnised. There were, however, six other places of Anglican worship. St. Andrew's was badly damaged in the air raid on 25th April 1942, and completely destroyed the following night by incendiary bombs. This view of the spire and west end is taken from Crescent Lane, which had three motor car establishments in 1930: William James Curtis, motor car proprietors, were at No. 16; opposite at No. 24 were Burcombe Brothers, motor engineers, advertising Regent British Petrol. The firm of William Tall & Son, motor car proprietors, were also trading from Crescent Lane, but are not shown on this postcard.

63. A group of idle boys watching the photographer about 1870 are leaning against the railings on the south side of Queen Square. Behind them looms John Wood the Elder's 1730s impressive north side designed as a single block, but consisting of seven houses, an early example of such a planned terrace. On the right is the east side of the Square, and Gay Street leading up to the Circus. The Square was Wood's first speculative development, and did not turn out quite as he wished, but is still one of Bath's finest Georgian designs. The obelisk, commissioned by Beau Nash to honour Frederick, Prince of Wales (George III's father), originally had a sharp point, but the tip was broken in a gale in 1815. Wood's formal parterres, gravel walks and stone balustrade were replaced by the lawns, trees and railings shown here.

64. The Francis Hotel started as Solomon Francis' lodginghouse and then became a private hotel. Here it occupies Nos. 6-11 of the south side of Queen Square. 'Electric light, garage and private motor bus' were some of the attractions which the proprietors E. Ponter & Sons advertised in 1928, the approximate date of the picture. The hotel suffered bomb damage in April 1942, but was rebuilt and extended in 1953 and is now a Trust House hotel. The inscription on the tablet on the right refers to the obelisk in the Square which was erected by Richard Nash in honour of Frederick Prince of Wales in 1738.

THE CIRCUS BATH, built by John Wood the Younger in the 18th century. Here at one time or other resided, Thackeray, Gainsborough, Livingstone, Lord Clive, the Earl of Chatham, and Parry the Arctic explorer.

THE CIRCUS BATH.

65. This aerial view of the Circus has Gay Street at the top, and a corner of the Assembly Rooms just visible at the left. It shows clearly the double mansard roofs, and the variations in each house behind the uniform façade designed by John Wood the Elder. The first stone laid was at William Pitt's pair of houses No. 7 and 8, in February 1754. Wood died three months later, and his son John the Younger supervised the rest of the development. Designed as three segments of a circle, comprising 33 houses each with a uniform frontage 42 feet high, made up of superimposed orders of Doric, Ionic and Corinthian pillars arranged in pairs, the King's Circus was Wood's masterpiece. He intended an open space in the centre, decorated with a statue of George II on horseback, but this did not materialise. In this picture it is just possible to see around the centre the 19th century railings which were removed during the war.

66. This card confidently claims No. 13 for Livingstone and 14 for Clive, but records show both men had probably stayed at No. 13 (although nearly a century apart). Robert Clive, hero of Plassey, first came to Bath in 1762, and took the 13th house in the Circus from 1768 to 1771. Lord Roberts unveiled a tablet to Clive at No. 14 in 1902, and was given the Freedom of the City, and a silver statuette of his (dead) V.C. son to mark the occasion. Dr. Livingstone stayed at No. 13 in September 1864 during the British Association Meeting, lecturing on his travels up the Zambesi. The meeting was devastated by the shooting of Speke at the height of his quarrel with Burton over the source of the Nile.

THE ROYAL CRESCENT BATH, built by John Wood the Younger in the 18th century is reputed the finest Crescent in England.

THE ROYAL CRESCENT, BATH   91464

67. Designed by John Wood the Younger, the Royal Crescent's full grandeur can best be seen from above. The foundation stone of No. 1, at the top of the picture, was laid in May 1767, but not until September 1778 were all thirty houses built and occupied. It is not strictly a crescent, but a concave semi-ellipse 538 feet across its axis, and 47 feet high. Each of the 114 Roman Ionic columns is 22 feet 6 inches high, and the ground storey face should be absolutely plain. However, as this photo shows, residents have planted climbing shrubs at the fronts of many of the houses, which spoil the effect. When the Crescent was being built, like other streets in Bath, leases were granted to individuals, who made their own arrangements for designing and building the houses behind the main façade. This is the reason for the differences of design at the backs of the buildings.

68. This photograph from the 1890s shows sheep grazing on the field in front of the Royal Crescent. It is unlikely that the residents will ever have anything except a green outlook, as the lawn belongs to them, and the Royal Victoria Park adjoins it. The house at the right is No. 1 which by an act of great generosity was given to Bath Preservation Trust in 1967 by the owner Major Bernard Cayzer. He also gave funds for the complete restoration and continuing maintenance of the house, which is now open to the public, showing what an 18th century town house would have been like.

69. The south side of the Assembly Rooms is seen here from Alfred Street in about 1907, with the not so glamorous rear of houses in the Circus on the left. Built by John Wood the Younger between 1768 and 1771, the 'Upper Rooms' were the venue for many splendid occasions. After a period of decline they were restored in 1938, when 19th century additions were removed. The building was gutted by an air raid in 1942. 1963 saw another reopening ceremony, after rebuilding and restoration by Sir Albert Richardson. In 1978 redecoration by Mr. David Mlinaric was carried out. In October 1987 the Assembly Rooms had to be closed as inherent faults affecting most of the plasterwork were discovered. A reopening is planned for 1991.

THE TEA ROOM, ASSEMBLY ROOMS, BATH.

70. The charge for tea was 6d extra at an Assembly Rooms ball, and was served in this pannelled tearoom with its four ornate fire-places and classic busts on pedestals between the columns. The view of about 1930 shows the two-tier row of columns with the gallery, meant for a small orchestra. Two of the three chandeliers are also shown. They escaped war damage and are at present being cleaned and restored, together with the other six chandeliers of the Rooms, in readiness for the reopening in 1991.

71. One of the best-known structures in Bath, the only Robert Adam design in the city, Pulteney Bridge was begun in 1769 to give William Pulteney easy access to his Bathwick estates across the Avon so that they could be developed. The bridge was not very sound: within ten years the lefthand pier was subsiding, and by 1804 the whole of that western end had to be rebuilt. What makes this bridge unusual is the row of little shops each side of the road. It has been compared with Palladio's design for the Venice Rialto Bridge, and the Ponte Vecchio in Florence, but it is not quite like either of them, and stands as an original design for Bath alone. In front of the bridge is the old weir, seen here about 1910 after the Grand Parade had been built on the colonnade at the left.

72. The general Committee for Promoting the Erection of Public Fountains in the City had earmarked six sites for fountains in 1850. Only the Laura Place project was carried out, to mark the Royal Bath & West of England Society's centenary in 1877. The unveiling ceremony on 14th July 1880 was attended by some ten thousand persons: about 4,000 participants of the Sunday School Centenary meeting on the same day swelled the numbers. Children from 16 Sunday Schools were lined up in the streets leading to Laura Place, carrying coloured banners. After the speeches and the National Anthem they marched off in procession with their teachers for a 'monster treat' at Weston.

73. This photograph shows the fountain in full play, thereby hiding most of the gothick details. The architect Alfred S. Goodridge was responsible for the design, and its 'elegance and simplicity' were much praised. The fountain had to be taken down in the 1940s because it was unsafe. In 1951 the fountain area was planted with flowers for the Festival of Britain. In 1960 the fountain was re-installed, but reduced in size. A new fountain was commissioned by the Bath & West Society in 1977 to commemorate their bicentenary. It was designed by the City Architect's Department and is made from Portland stone.

74. No. 1, Johnstone Street, seen here just behind the waiting broughams, was built in 1789 as part of Laura Place, but the rest of the street was not completed until about 1805, fifteen years later. This part of William Johnstone Pulteney's planned development on his wife's Bathwick estate was delayed by the failure of the Bath City Bank in 1793. The carriages are standing beside the cabbies' shelter, put up in the 1890s for the benefit of the drivers, and taken down in 1963 because by then taxis no longer operated from Laura Place.

Henrietta Park, Bath.

75. This postcard showing Henrietta Park was posted on 11th January 1907. It is now impossible to see any buildings from the photographer's viewpoint: mature trees have closed the vista. The seven acres for the park were given by Captain Forester, a great nephew of the last Duke of Cleveland and heir to the Bathwick estate. Councillor Morris designed the park and daily supervised the work in progress. A contemporary report praised him as 'one of the busiest and most useful of our public men'. The opening was on 22nd June 1897 during Queen Victoria 's Diamond Jubilee Week. In the summer of 1908 an alfresco tea garden was opened at the Bathwick Street end of the park. The enterprising businessman was Mr. A. Ernest Meyer, confectioner of New Bond Street. A wooden building with rustic trellis work was erected as a shelter from sudden rain. Further plans included a croquet lawn and tennis court.

PULTENEY STREET, BATH.

76. The length (1,100 feet = 335 metres) and width (100 feet = 30 metres) of Great Pulteney Street impresses in this view, taken about 1930 from the Holburne of Menstrie Museum looking towards Laura Place. Thomas Baldwin designed the street as part of the new Bathwick development about 1788. The whole plan was never carried out, as the collapse of Bath City Bank in 1793 meant bankruptcy for Baldwin and other builders. The trees have been cut down to improve the view of the architecture and stone cleaning has given the façades a facelift in recent years. The original purpose of the 'watchmen's boxes' and their date is uncertain. They are still there, whilst the decorative railings were taken down in the latter years of the Second World War.

GREAT PULTENEY STREET, BATH.

77. This view of about 1912 looking towards the Holburne Museum shows horse-drawn cabs near the shelter and in front of the Pulteney Hotel, together with a motor car, ready to pick up customers. This luxurious hotel was established by Mr. Stead about 1866 at Nos. 1 and 2 Pulteney Street and later extended to include Nos. 4-6 Laura Place. The Admiralty requisitioned the hotel in 1942, and when it was finally vacated in 1978, it was converted into apartments. It is now known as Connaught Mansions.

ST. MARYS CHURCH, BATHWICK. 2538.

M.J.R.B.

78. The photograph of St. Mary's Church was taken from Pulteney Road long before the roundabout was built to slow down the traffic. Here only one carriage is in sight. John Pinch the Elder, surveyor on the Earl of Darlington's estate in Bathwick, was the architect of St. Mary's. 1,000 tickets for admission were distributed when it was consecrated in 1820. It was planned to dedicate the church to St. Paul, as there was already an old St. Mary's Church in the parish, but its condition, already very poor, deteriorated further, and it had to be demolished before the consecration of the new church took place.

79. This view shows the interior of St. Mary's looking east. The original altarpiece for the church was a nativity scene, painted by the local artist Benjamin Barker and acquired for £160.6.10d. It was later moved to the west wall, and the present carved altarpiece took its place. It has been dated as early 16th century and is probably Dutch.

REV. H. M. SCARTH M.A.,
Rector of Bathwick.

80. A window in St. Mary's, Bathwick was erected to the Reverend H.M. Scarth's memory by public subscription. He had been rector of St. Mary's for thirty years, when in 1871 he accepted the living of Wrington, as he wanted a quieter life with less responsibility and more time for his research: he was an authority on Roman antiquities. Besides his parish duties at St. Mary's he managed to sift, collect and arrange much scattered material on the relics of the Roman occupation in the Bath area. He was not known as an eloquent preacher, but visible signs of his work at St. Mary's were the chancel, built during his time, and the formation of Bathwick Cemetery at Smallcombe.

81. The houses at Dunsford Place on the lower slopes of Bathwick Hill were built about 1825 as part of the new residential development beyond Pulteney Bridge. This 1930s view shows St. Mary's at the bottom of the hill, St. Swithin's behind it, and St. Stephen's and the slopes of Lansdown in the background. Camden Crescent and the arches supporting the road in front of it can be clearly seen.

RABY PLACE

82. When it was first built about 1825, Raby Place was called Church Street; the name was changed between 1829 and 1833. John Pinch the Elder (about 1770-1827) was surveyor of the Bathwick estate for the Earl of Darlington. He designed several of the terraced houses on the slopes of Bathwick Hill, among them was Raby Place. Looking at this peaceful traffic-free view − no roundabout at the bottom of the hill − one finds it hard to believe that at approximately the time this picture was taken, in 1928, the owner-occupiers of Raby Place complained about heavy traffic in a petition they presented to the Corporation. They feared that the cellars of their houses, which extended to the middle of the roadway, might get damaged. The Corporation's decision was that they could not accept liability for the owners' cellars...

83. This picture, taken from the bridge on Bathwick Hill, shows Sydney Wharf on the Kennet and Avon Canal. From here guns were fired to celebrate when, after a long delay, on 10th November 1810 the locks at Bath were opened to traffic. During the following prosperous years this wharf like the others on the Bath stretch of the canal saw much commercial activity. The competition of the railway proved too strong eventually, and the Kennet & Avon Canal committee made an offer to the GWR. The transfer was authorised in 1852. Almost 100 years later restoration work started, and the canal is now once more navigable. The ashlar and timber building was demolished some time after 1964, the site is now a car park for British Gas employees. The corrugated shed − the first structure on the left − is still there, though without its BELCO sign. Other buildings on the wharf have been converted into attractive cottages, and pleasure craft are now moored here.

St. John the Baptist.   Bath.

84. On 24th June St. John the Baptist's Day in 1861, the foundation stone for this church was laid. It was meant for the 'poorer brethren' in the district, as St. Mary's already served residents in the new Bathwick area. The site was given by Lord William Powlett. The architect was C.E. Giles, the builder George Mann. It looked a rather small insignificant building for some years, as tower and spire were only added three years later. For lighting and heating £11 a year were set aside, but by 1869 costs had risen to £61, and the choir expenses amounted to £166. They included the cost of 'Bridge Tickets': Cleveland Bridge had been built to replace the ferry, and until 1929 a toll of ½d was charged to all foot passengers.

85. Worship at St. John's had always been in the more Catholic tradition of the Anglican church. At the end of the 19th century this led to a long-drawn-out argument between the parish priest and the Bishop of the diocese, who did not approve of certain rituals being used in the service. Eventually a ban was placed on St. John's: there would be no visit by the Bishop; he would not license any curate, nor would the parish priest be allowed to present any candidates for confirmation. A new bishop finally, in 1920, ended the ban and made peace with the new vicar and the parish. At his first visit the congregation presented him with a mitre as a token of their gratitude.

Interior St. John
The Baptist. Bath.
10 757

86. The terraced houses on the right are Waterloo Buildings. Together with part of Ebenezer Terrace, shown further along, they were demolished in 1969, when the new traffic scheme at Widcombe was carried out. The next building, Ebenezer Chapel, erected in 1820 and now Widcombe Baptist Church, is well-known for its roof inscription. The rescue and renovation of the Widcombe flight of locks were part of the canal re-development which was completed in 1976. It was the construction of the locks in Bath which delayed the opening of the canal in 1810. Several locks are so near to each other that 'large side ponds were required, lined on their sides and ends with stone'.

87. Charles Harcourt Masters, surveyor and architect, son of a local goldsmith, built Widcombe Terrace around 1805 in a 'back to front' design: the back doors of the houses face the street, the front doors at the back are reached over a terrace, from which there is a splendid view of the valley. Hardly any change has taken place here since this picture was taken on a sunny summer's day around 1930.

88. As one of the last of the great Georgian terraces in Bath, this row of 19 houses was built in 1826. There are pediments on the end houses and the centre portion, and balconies on the first floor windows. Front gardens, a stream and trees separate the houses from the road and give them a special charm. The date of this postcard is about 1930.

89. An 1829 drawing by Thomas H. Shepherd is the original for this view of St. Mary Magdalen, the chapel on the old pilgrim's route to Glastonbury. A hospice for pilgrims was built near it and later became a leper hospital. Prior Cantlow carried out major repairs to the chapel in 1495: an inscription in the porch documents this. Before St. Mark's was built in 1820, Lyncombe was dependent on St. Mary Magdalen as a church. It was restored in the 1930s and again after bomb damage in 1942. The Hospital, seen on the right, was rebuilt in 1761. It used to be a children's home until earlier this century. The Judas tree near the porch still delights residents and visitors with its crimson blossoms each spring time.

LYNCOMBE VALE BATH

90. This view of pleasant villas in Lyncombe Vale, with the raised walk along the brook, has hardly changed since it was taken around 1930. The seat has gone, though. According to a resident, it used to be a favourite resting place for the local policeman on his round. The bank was once covered with daisies and might have given its name to the row of terraced houses at the entrance of this road – Daisybank. The tall conifer was in the garden of No. 5 Sunny Bank, owned by Mrs. Fuller in 1930. The tree had to be taken down in the 1950s having reached the height of circa 30 ft.

91. The arch at the top of Pope's Lane or Blind Lane is still there. The footpath leads from Perrymead to Carriage Drive and is used as a short cut today, as it was then by the schoolboys on this postcard. The arch was known as Shepherd's Arch, or − more sinister − Hangman's Arch. Peter Coard suggests that the latter might be a corruption of 'Hanging Land Lane', which was another old name for the path.

10008-1 BATH. WIDCOMBE CHURCH. ROTARY PHOTO. E.C.

92. The west end of St. Thomas à Beckett and the south front of Widcombe Manor are shown on this postcard of about 1912. The manor was then occupied by the Misses Firth; later and until his death in 1955 it was the home of Horace Annesley Vachell, a prolific writer. The house features in one of his novels as 'Golden House' and older residents still call it so. The church stands on the site of much older places of worship. There was a Saxon chapel here, then a Norman church. The present church was rebuilt by prior Cantlow. He died in 1499 before the project was finished. He put his mark on every building he erected or restored: in Widcombe his coat of arms is on the north side of the tower.

Fly-leaf of Old Anglo-Saxon Gospel Book in use
in Widcombe in the time of the Conqueror.

For details see Guide Books, to be obtained at the Church,
or at the Herald Office, Bath.

Proceeds for the Church.

93. The Anglo-Saxon text on this postcard is a reproduction of the flyleaf of a pre-983 gospel book, which was used in the Saxon chapel at Widcombe. When Anglo-Saxon was no longer understood, the book was returned to the monastery and eventually presented to Corpus Christi College at Cambridge, where it still is. The second and third paragraphs of this text refer to transactions between a resident of Lyncombe and the abbot around the year 1080.

BATH FROM THE MONUMENT FIELD
COMBE DOWN

94. Taken from an unusual angle this shows Bath from Combe Down, south-east of the city. The particular viewpoint is the Monument Field, where Bishop Warburton and his wife Gertrude erected a monument to her uncle Ralph Allen. Among the trees at the bottom is Widcombe Church, and part of the farm adjacent to it, although Widcombe Manor itself is completely hidden by the trees. Across the centre between the Empire Hotel and Walcot Church is the imposing view of the back of The Paragon. Pulteney Bridge and Weir can be seen almost in the centre. The top right quarter contains Camden Crescent, above the arches in Hedgemead Park, and further up Lansdown stand the Royal School and Kingswood School. The spire on the left above the Abbey belongs to St. Andrew's Church, and was 240 feet from the ground to the tip. It was a well-known landmark, until destroyed in the 1942 air raids.

Prior Park, Bath. 1654.

95. This view of Prior Park shows the main front with the impressive steps, colonnades and church. Ralph Allen's mansion designed by Wood and partly built by him, was finished by Richard Jones, Allen's clerk of works. Many alterations have taken place since. The church was added in 1844 after a design by Joseph Scoles. Because of serious financial difficulties, work had to be stopped in 1856 and was only begun again in 1872, this time by the designer's son, Alexander Joseph Cory Scoles.
When this view was taken about 1912 Prior Park was still owned by the Catholic Church and used for various educational purposes. It became a boys' boarding school in 1924, run by the Congregation of Christian Brothers. It is now a boarding – and day – school for boys and girls, run by the laity whilst retaining its Catholic character.

96. Reverend Mgr. Edward Williams (1831-1891) went to Prior Park as a 13 year old pupil, and began his theological studies there. In 1855 the College closed and he continued his training in Rome. He was headmaster of Clifton Catholic Grammar School, when the Bishop and his Canons decided to repurchase Prior Park. The school moved back to Bath from 'confined and crowded rooms to large and lofty halls, and ample space for recreation'. Williams' personality and his musical talents made his period as headmaster a successful one for the school. After his death funds were collected in his memory to build an up-to-date gymnasium on the site of the former Drill Hall which had been a wooden structure. This chair at the Milsom Street studio, where his portrait was taken, was obviously reserved for the clergy among the clients of Flukes, the photographers.

97. The model for the famous Palladian Bridge at Prior Park was the one at Wilton, erected for the 9th Earl of Pembroke in his grounds in 1735-1737. The Prior Park bridge stems from 1755. This panoramic postcard of about 1920 shows how much its structure against a background of trees and water enhances the view from the mansion. Crowe Hall and parts of Manor Farm (the dovecote?) are visible in the distance. There are at present plans for the National Trust to take over and maintain the grounds at Prior Park. The public would then have access to parts of 'Mr. Allen's gardens' and enjoy this famous view.

A PEEP THROUGH SHAM CASTLE. BATH.

98. St. Swithin's, Walcot can be seen on the left, and Camden Crescent in the centre of this view, taken about 1930 through one of the arches of Sham Castle. The 40 feet high and 100 feet long Folly was built for Ralph Allen in 1762. It was to form part of the vista from his town house, but Allen also wanted to prove that Bath stone was a perfectly good material to use, 'durable, beautiful and cheap'. The original design is probably by the architect Sanderson Miller, but Ralph Allen's clerk of works, Richard Jones, claimed to have built it. Sham Castle was given to the city in 1921. The stonework has recently been skilfully restored without spoiling the 'ruin' impression. Floodlit at night, it forms an interesting landmark.

99. Richard Jones designed the monument for Ralph Allen's Tomb in Claverton. When the foundations for it were dug, four skeletons were found. By their uniforms they were identified as soldiers killed in the Battle of Claverton 1643. Ralph Allen spent much time at Claverton Manor, which he bought in 1758. He used to drive over from Prior Park once a week and was a generous benefactor to the village church. The gallery which he presented to it was used for the first time at his funeral on 5th July 1764. In 1976 the roof of the tomb had fallen in, and the local paper reported: 'Soon Ralph could have a tomb with a view.' Since then extensive restoration has taken place and a marble plaque has been added commemorating 'Ralph Allen 1693-1764, responsible for the establishment of Cross Posts'.

Monument near Prior Park, Bath.
Erected by Bishop Warburton to the Memory of his predecessor at Prior Park, Ralph Allen, who died in 1764.

100. William Warburton, Bishop of Gloucester, married Ralph Allen's niece and inherited Prior Park. Out of gratitude he designed this monument himself. One cannot feel regret that it does not adorn the 'Monument field' at Combe Down, to which it gave its name, anymore. The shape of the base was triangular, perhaps as an allusion to the Holy Trinity. A Latin inscription over the door commemorated Ralph Allen. The round tower had a circular staircase with 75 steps. The view from the top must have been splendid and the only justification for this bizarre design. The monument was finally pulled down in 1953 at a cost of £600. It had been inaccessible to the public for many years before this date.

North Road,
Combe Down.

101. The Bathford to Combe Down tramline was completed in 1904 after an argument over road widening had been settled. Tram No. 34 stops here in front of Stanley Villas and Ferley, now 65 and 67 North Road. St. Kilda Villas, now Della Rosa Guesthouse and Moresby Villas are the houses on the left. At the end of the green on the right is the Hadley Arms, where Mr. Farnham Flower was the innkeeper at the time of the picture, about 1910. The card, incidentally, was sent on 15th August 1968 to the Lending Library at Bridge Street asking for the renewal of two library books.

102. Parishioners gathered on a wet day, when the Bishop of Bath and Wells laid the foundation stone for a new church in South Twerton in 1906. The event took place on Ascension Day − 24th May − as the church was to be called 'Church of the Ascension'. In 1907, again on Ascension Day, the dedication of the nave took place, and the Bishop again officiated.

103. Five years later, and another Ascension Day – 25th May 1911 – in South Twerton: the foundation stone of the chancel is at last being laid. There was a full Masonic ceremony, with a procession of Masons from South Twerton School to the site. The stone was laid by the Provincial Grand Master of Somerset, Col. William Long, C.M.G., with a silver trowel which had last been used when the foundation stone of the Albert Memorial wing of the Royal United Hospital was laid. The Bishop of Bath and Wells is seen here offering the dedication prayer.

CLAUDE AVENUE, BATH (SHOWING CHURCH OF ASCENSION).

104. This 1930s view shows Claude Avenue in South Twerton with the church on the right. The building was finally completed and consecrated on 2nd December 1911 and became a separate parish church with its own vicar. The first one was Reverend Pryce Davies.

= LAYING OF FOUNDATION STONE =
- TWERTON ELEMENTARY SCHOOL -
BY JONATHAN CARR ESQ 19 DEC 1910

105. Mr. Jonathan Carr of Wood House, Twerton, is the centre one of the three bearded gentlemen in this picture. He had come to the village as a boy of 13 in 1853, when his father Isaac took over the Twerton Cloth Mills. Jonathan Carr was a benefactor to the church and parish of Twerton, but education was his particular concern. He contributed generously towards establishing this Higher Elementary School in Twerton. It later became Twerton Secondary Modern, and was then used by Culverhay School. The building at Lymore Avenue is now Bath Teachers' Centre, and still has the plaque commemorating the occasion shown in this postcard. Though the weather was not very favourable for the stone laying ceremony on this December day in 1910, a large crowd had gathered.

106. A tablet was unveiled on this house in Twerton in 1909 — about nine years after the date of this photograph — claiming that Henry Fielding lived here whilst he was writing 'Tom Jones'. The author definitely stayed here at Fielding's Lodge with his wife in 1743, but the earliest documentary evidence that he was working on 'Tom Jones' — then entitled 'The Foundling' — stems from 1747. The book was published in 1749. Fielding was a frequent visitor to Bath. His marriage to Charlotte Craddock took place in Charlcombe Church in 1734, and Charlotte died in Bath in 1744. Fielding's Lodge apparently was a comfortable, even luxurious dwelling, which stood in an acre of ground. It had stables, a fish pond and an orchard. It was demolished in 1963.

Twerton on Avon, Bath.

107. This view of Twerton High Street was taken from the railway bridge about 1905 and shows part of the platform. Twerton still had its own station then: it was closed in 1917. The picture shows how the construction of the railway virtually cut the village of Twerton in half. On the left are − then and now − the houses numbered 158-153. The taller white house on the corner of Shophouse Road is now used by Office Economy. The wall on the right, here covered with posters, shows now an inscription in old lettering: 'Bath Co-operative Society. Join now. 6d entrance fee.' It may well have been there at the time of the photograph, underneath the posters.

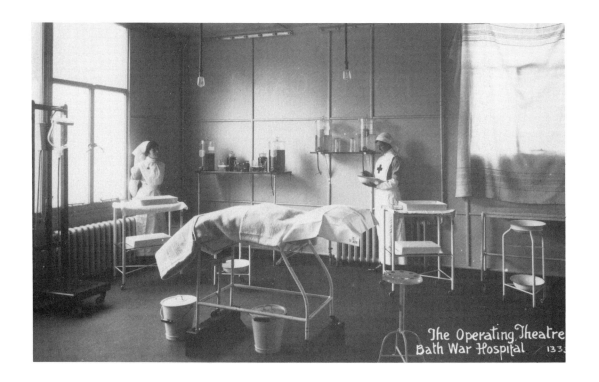

The Operating Theatre
Bath War Hospital 133

108. In May 1915 the War Office asked Bath City to provide a 500 bed hospital for wounded frontline soldiers. By April 1916 it was ready: a corridor 800 feet long with ten wards leading from it, and other facilities including a dispensary, an X-ray unit and this spartan operating theatre. The sheet has B.W.H.T. stencilled or embroidered on the corner denoting Bath War Hospital Theatre. An adjustable table, trolleys, anaesthetic equipment, bright lights, bowls, buckets, instruments and a dedicated staff: what more could be expected in such a short time!

Bath
War Hospital
1332
WARD Nº 10.

109. Some of the soldiers in the picture seem hardly old enough to join the army. On the table behind the front three patients are bottles of medicine: probably dispensed in the hospital dispensary, which was organised on a voluntary basis by E. Whiston, of Hawes, Whiston & Co., 37 St. Jame's Square, together with a team of other volunteer chemists from Bath. The snowy white sheets were laundered by a team of volunteers supervised by Mrs. Maynard, and Mrs. Bannatyne, wives respectively of the Vicar of Twerton and the Hospital Commandant. These wards were made of corrugated iron and asbestos, and were slightly less spartan than the tents which housed an extra 500 men. Each ward had fifty patients. Visitors were allowed on Tuesdays, Thursdays and Sundays: perhaps the lady in the felt hat at the back was someone's mother visiting her wounded son.

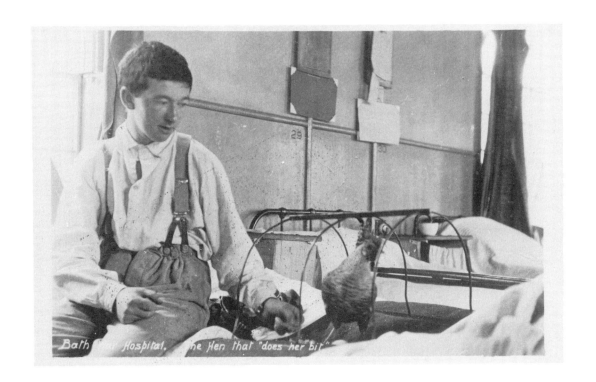

Bath ... Hospital, ...he Hen that "does her bit"

110. One of the more curious stories to be told about Bath War Hospital was of the hen that lived in a coop made from a bed cradle, and laid a daily egg on the bed of a wounded soldier in Ward 10. Someone even wrote a verse about her: 'Our hospital hen, Goes to Ward Number 10. If you want to know when It lays eggs − ask the men.' Not great poetry! The hen appears to have been a Plymouth Rock, having grey feathers banded with black. As no dogs were allowed in the hospital she was the nearest thing to a pet for the patients.

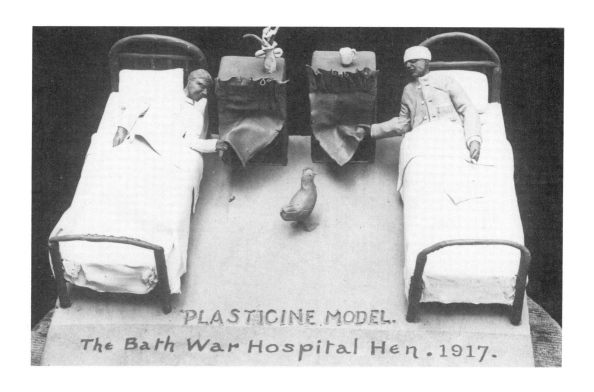

PLASTICINE MODEL.
The Bath War Hospital Hen. 1917.

111. So famous was the Hospital Hen, that in 1917 somebody created a model in plasticine to celebrate her activities. William Harbutt was an art teacher in Bath, who developed plasticine as a clean, pliable modelling clay for his students. He and his daughter Olive travelled around the world demonstrating its uses, and it is possible that this model may have been made by one of the Harbutts. The firm existed at Bathampton from 1900 to 1983.

112. The name above the building declares it to be the Bath, Somerset and Wilts Central Children's Orthopaedic Hospital, as it would have been about 1926. Opened in May 1924 by the Duke of Connaught at the same time as the Forbes Fraser Hospital nearby, it was originally called the Children's Orthopaedic Hospital. The buildings were reputedly two converted First World War aeroplane hangars from the Midlands. The south side of each ward was completely open throughout the year: temperature extremes of 104°F and 8°F were recorded, and nursing staff normally wore outdoor clothes during the winter. Many of the young patients stayed for several years, and were only allowed visits from parents on two days a month. There were some treats, however, as Evans' Fish Restaurant regularly supplied fish and chips on Bonfire Night (5th November); and this photo shows that there were dedicated nurses to care for the children, and at least one enormous teddy bear, here being bandaged like a patient.

THE WAR MEMORIAL. BATH.

113. After considering 18 different sites, and a delay of several years, Bath's Memorial to the dead of the Great War was unveiled at the entrance to the Royal Victoria Park on 3rd November 1927. The bronze tablets, which listed about a thousand citizens who had died, were donated by the Mayor Cedric Chivers, designed by Henry Poole, cast by Singers of Frome, and originally fixed to the wall of the Mineral Water Hospital in April 1923. The Mayor donated another £300, and 5,000 others subscribed to the total cost of about £3,000 for the Memorial proper. His Worship also consented to moving his bronzes to join the Cross of Sacrifice at the new site. Sadly he was too ill to attend the unveiling, and Lord Allenby was asked to officiate.

Victoria Park, Bath.

114. The local paper described the 11 year old Princess Victoria as 'a sweet and engaging child' when she visited Bath in 1830 and named the newly created Park 'Royal Victoria'. The park had been formed from common land belonging to the Bath Freemen. The obelisk, designed by Bath architect G.P. Manners, was intended to celebrate Victoria's 18th birthday, but the official opening was postponed to coincide with her coronation on 28th June 1838. In 1857 the government presented Bath with two Russian cannons, captured in 1855 at Sebastapol in the Crimea: one can just be seen on the left of the three seated children. These guns remained a popular feature near the obelisk until 1941, when they were removed for use as scrap: the loot of one war went to fight another. This photo may have been taken during the Bath Pageant in 1909 as the long dresses of two ladies near the right seem too elaborate for normal outdoor wear compared with other people in the picture.

Wembley Pavilion, Bath

"Westfield" 291

115. In February 1924 Bath Corporation decided to take a site at the British Empire Exhibition at Wembley later that year to publicize the city. The exhibit took the form of a model of the Roman Baths, and this little building. The exhibit cost the ratepayers just over £2,115, but was good value, as many tourists, and even new residents, came to Bath after seeing such an attractive advertisement at Wembley. At the end of 1925 the Pavilion was brought back to Bath and re-erected on a site acquired for the purpose at the north-east corner of the Botanic Gardens, where it remains to this day as a shelter and vantage point for visitors to the gardens in the park. Just visible to the right of the wall is the spire of St. Andrew's. The church was built in 1873, but the spire only added in 1879.

116. When Sir John Miller and Lady Miller returned from their Grand Tour, they brought this stone vase as a souvenir back to their home near Bath. The vase, found in 1769 near Frascati in Italy, was given a new purpose at Lady Miller's weekly literary breakfasts at Batheaston Villa. Guests at these gatherings were invited to write poems on a specific subject, and to complete a set of given rhymes. The results were deposited in the vase and read out by the gentlemen of the party in turn. Four volumes of these 'Poetical Amusements at a villa near Bath' were published between 1775 and 1781. The poor benefitted from the pastime of the idle rich: the profits of the books went to the Pauper Charity of Bath, of which Sir John Miller was president. The vase eventually found a home in the Victoria Park. It stands now — without its pillared cover — between the putting green and the shelter.

GRANVILLE MONUMENT, LANSDOWN

117. Erected in 1720 by Lord Lansdown in memory of his grandfather Sir Bevil Granville (or Grenville) near the spot where the latter died in 1643 on Lansdown hill, this monument has the heraldic griffin, crest of the Granvilles on the top. The inscription on the upper front is a quotation from Clarendon's 'History', and (seen here) on the upper back are verses describing Sir Bevil's exploits. John Wood the Elder described the monument meticulously, including a local joke about miserly John Harvey, the carver who was paid by the Granvilles but never paid his own workman for his labour. Among the other carvings – coats of arms, military symbols and details of the many repairs – are unofficial inscriptions: the earliest graffito said: 'G.M. 1721.'

118. The North Somerset Imperial Yeomanry, descended from a force originally formed in the Napoleonic Wars, had often been called since then to quell local riots. Their drill ground at Bath was the Lansdown Race Course, and a series of postcards was produced to commemorate the May 1905 Training Camp. The regiment had served in the 1900/01 South African War, and probably many of the men (and horses?) at this camp had been there, or would be involved in the next war in 1914.

N.S. IY. LANSDOWN CAMP 1905

119. The Yeomanry commenced training on 10th May 1905, and on 20th they were ready for inspection by Lord Roberts. He was at the time not only a Freeman of Bath, but also a member of the Committee of Imperial Defence. However, he resigned from the latter six months later: he had advocated National Service for home defence, but the Committee did not agree with him.

Cavendish Place, Bath. 559

120. This row of terraced houses was designed by John Pinch the Elder as one of several on the slopes of Lansdown and the first to be built, from 1808 to 1815. The view of about 1930 gives a good impression of the pleasing architecture of these thirteen houses built on the steeply rising hill. They are facing west and overlook the High Common, now the Approach Golf Course.

Camden Crescent. Bath. 947.

121. What is now known as Camden Crescent was originally called Upper Camden Place and is only part of a much larger project. Work on it had to be stopped because of serious landslides. Only the houses built on solid rock were finished, others were eventually demolished. Camden Crescent was named after Charles Pratt, 1st Earl of Camden, politician and Recorder of Bath. The tympanon in the central building shows his coat of arms and his crest, an elephant's head, appears on the keystones of the doorways. In 1765 the Corporation commissioned a full length portrait of Sir Charles. 'For picture and frame' the painter William Hoare was paid £84. It now hangs in the Banqueting Room of the Guildhall.

Belvedere, Bath.

122. This card, posted in 1906, shows the handsome block, Nos. 1 and 2 Belvedere, Lansdown Road, built in the mid-1770s by an unidentified architect. From 1908 the two houses were owned by the Bath Eye Infirmary. This institution had a chequered history, starting in 1811 in Bath Street as one of the earliest eye hospitals in the country outside London, and moving from one building to another several times in the next fifty years. From 1861 until 1889 it occupied No. 2 Belvedere. In 1889 the Infirmary bought the premises at No. 1 and left No. 2, which became a Hospital for Fallen Women for several years. From 1904 until 1908 No. 2 was again a private house, but then was bought by the Eye Infirmary to join up with No. 1. The two houses remained in use as the Bath Eye Hospital until 1973 when the buildings were converted into flats and the patients moved to the Royal United Hospital at Combe Park.

123. This view of the west end and tower of St. Stephen's was taken about 1912 from Lansdown Road, on a sunny afternoon at 20 minutes past one, with a char-à-banc waiting to take parishioners for an outing. The foundation stone of St. Stephen's was laid in 1840, and the cost of building estimated to be £2,000, but the church was only consecrated in 1889. This was due to a disagreement with the church authorities who did not approve of the siting of the altar. Substantial building alterations were needed, but the money ran out, and no consecration could take place until the church was free of debt... From 1845 to 1889 St. Stephen's was licensed as a Chapel of Ease to Walcot, but at the consecration it became a parish church with its own incumbent and independent of Walcot. The architect was James Wilson who is buried at Lansdown cemetery.

St. Stephens Church, Lansdown, Bath

Royal Military College for Officers' Daughters. Lansdown, Bath. 1078.

124. The building on Lansdown for the 'School for Daughters of Officers of the Army' was bought by a Committee in 1863 and the first thirty pupils moved in on 24th August 1865. The large school complex had been designed by the architect James Wilson for the Bath and Lansdown Proprietary College, a boys' day school which failed a few years after it was set up. This postcard shows the Royal School about 1900. The new wing, jutting out to the east, was added in 1883, during Miss Walker's time as Lady Superintendent. The extension, built of the same stone and in the same style as the original building, also shows the school's initials over the dormer windows.

125. The plans for this extension to the Royal School were well-advanced when the First World War broke out. The foundation stone was finally laid in 1924 and the opening took place on 3rd July 1925. It provided the school with much needed extra classrooms and a two-storey high Memorial Hall. The ground floor originally contained an art room, cloakrooms, and a playroom with open arches. During the Admiralty's stay at the school in the Second World War, these arches were fitted with doors to create more space. The designer of the building was Mowbray A. Green (1865-1945), head of a local firm of architects and surveyors. He was an authority on Georgian architecture and the author of 'Eighteenth century architecture of Bath', which is still a standard work.

126. At his arrival in Bath William Beckford immediately purchased land at the rear of Lansdown Crescent stretching to the top of the hill. Henry Edmund Goodridge, son of a Bathwick builder, designed this tower for Beckford in 1827, having already built a bridge to connect his two houses in the Crescent. Goodridge's connection with Lansdown continued: he designed the entrance archway to the cemetery in 1848 and was buried here in 1864. Beckford used the tower as a retreat and filled it with pieces from his large collection of furniture, pictures, porcelain, books, vases, bronzes, and Chinese and Japanese lacquer. The tower and the cemetery around it later became property of the church. In 1971 the tower was saved from further deterioration by Elizabeth and Leslie Hilliard, who bought and restored it. It is now run by a trust and houses a Beckford Museum.

Lansdown Cemetery. Bath. 1046

127. The cemetery at Lansdown owes its existence to William Beckford, who wanted to be buried near his tower, seen in the background, and near his dog. As the ground was not consecrated, he was buried, in 1844, in Lyncombe Vale. In 1848 his daughter, Lady Hamilton, presented the ground near the tower to the parish of Walcot, and Beckford's remains were re-interred under the pink granite tomb which he had designed himself. The roofed tomb in the centre of this postcard of about 1912 is the burial ground of the Wilson family. James Wilson, FSA, the well-known Bath architect, who died on 19th May 1900, is buried here. The flat topped tomb behind, now almost hidden by trees, is Samuel Humphrey Pellew's of Falmouth, who died in 1854. The third distinctive monument in the picture, now without its top ornament, is the grave of Dame Ann Hussey Bickerton, widow of Admiral Sir Richard Hussey Bickerton.

REV. W.H. POWELL, M.A.

INCUMBENT OF ALL SAINTS. BATH.

128. Like other chapels in Bath in the 18th century All Saints was built by individual initiative and by subscription. Pew rents provided the funds for renumerating the clergy and maintaining the building. The chapels remained the property of the builders, hence the term 'proprietary chapel'. A church in the Lansdown area was needed for residents and visitors in this newly developed part of Bath. John Palmer was the architect and Thomas Barker designed altar piece and ornaments. The church was opened for worship on 26th October 1794. It was situated on a steep slope above Park Street towards Lansdown Crescent. A feature of the building was the dwelling house underneath the chapel. Reverend W.H. Powell was minister from 1903 to 1907. All Saints was destroyed in the air raid on Bath on 26th April 1942.

129. This view from the lower slopes of Lansdown towards Charlcombe shows Barn House in the foreground and the church on the left. The square bell turret with two openings and battlements is clearly visible, also the giant yew to the south-west of the church. The writer Henry Fielding was married here, and his sister Sarah was buried in the cemetery. According to tradition the history of St. Mary the Virgin, Charlcombe, goes back further than that of the Abbey. The rectory – the large house set back from the road near the church – was sold in 1988, and at this time Wansdyke Planning Department received a rather unique application. It concerned the move of a holy well from the rectory garden to a new site in the adjacent Church Field. Permission was granted, the well was re-sited and re-dedicated in September 1989.

CHARLCOMBE BATH.

St. Catherine's Church

130. St. Catherine's Church and Court in Batheaston had strong links with the Benedictine monastery of Bath. The Court retains relics of the grange which belonged to Bath Abbey and may date back to Prior Cantlow's time, i.e. the late 15th century. The tower of the little church was rebuilt in 1704. Much restoration work was carried out in 1975. Its outward appearance now – apart from minor changes – is the same as on the view of about 1930, including the sundial.

PRIOR JOHN CANTLOW,
(from a contemporary portrait).
He built Widcombe Parish Church, and died
A.D. 1499.

For further particulars see Guide Book.

131. One of the four 15th century east windows in St. Catherine's Church has this portrait of John Cantlow in a kneeling position. In 1489 he was sacristan of the monastery at Bath and was elected by the convent to be prior. He became a generous restorer of churches and ecclesiastical buildings. The chancel at St. Catherine's was built or rebuilt by him. A brass of Prior Cantlow, based on this portrait, is at the chancel wall of St. Thomas à Beckett Widcombe.

Bathampton.

132. There is a precise date for this picture of Bathampton High Street: it was taken in 1912, when Ted Dolman was nine years old; he is the boy on the right, and still lives in the village. The horse and cart belonged to farmer Candy, for whom Ted Dolman later worked for many years. Yew Tree Cottage had then two yew trees in front of it, one is still standing. Tythe Cottage on the right was then known as the Old Barn and was used as a Working Men's Club. Later, a member of the Harbutt family lived there and had a window put in, facing High Street, for a display of Harbutt's goods. The window was blocked up again, and the lintel is still visible.

Bathampton.

133. The iron gate posts and the gate are still at the entrance of the right hand lane leading to the railway line. Bathampton station – on the main line of the Great Western Railway – and the goods yard used to be at the bottom of the lane. The Schoolhouse and the Station House still exist. The farm buildings in the lefthand lane have recently been converted into cottages.

The Canal. Bathampton.

134. This picture of the bridge over the Kennet and Avon Canal at Bathampton was taken around 1912 from the George Inn. The boy has probably just left school and is strolling home along the bank. Part of the schoolhouse can be seen on the left, and also the gable of the school with its turret. The school was built in 1896 and has recently been renovated and extended, but the front facing the lane is unchanged with the bell still hanging in its bell-gable.

Bathampton Bridge

135. Another view of the bridge, this time looking towards the inn, with some of the cottages at Chapel Row peeping through the arch. The playing fields of King Edward's School are now alongside Dark Lane, where the very elaborate haystacks can be seen in this picture. The card is stamped 6th July 1905 at 9.15.

IN MEMORY OF
ADMIRAL ARTHUR PHILLIP·R·N·
FOUNDER AND FIRST GOVERNOR
OF
AUSTRALIA

BORN IN LONDON 11 OCTOBER 1738
ENTERED THE ROYAL NAVY 1755
DIED AT 19 BENNETT STREET BATH
31 AUGUST 1814

TO HIS INDOMITABLE COURAGE PROPHETIC VISION
FORBEARANCE FAITH INSPIRATION AND WISDOM
WAS DUE THE SUCCESS OF THE FIRST SETTLEMENT
IN AUSTRALIA AT SYDNEY
26 JANUARY 1788

THE EARTH IS THE LORD'S AND THE FULLNESS THEREOF
CORINTHIANS X·26

ADMIRAL PHILLIP MEMORIAL IN THE NORTH CHOIR OF
THE BATH ABBEY.

136. In Bath Admiral Phillip is commemorated by this tablet in the Abbey and by the Australia Chapel in Bathampton Church. Each year a ceremony is held in his memory at his grave in Bathampton. After his return from Australia, Admiral Phillip eventually settled in Bath, hoping his poor health might benefit from the waters. A national memorial was in the parish of his birth, the Church of St. Mildred, Bread Street, London, but it was destroyed in the Second World War. There were plans to establish a museum and Australian Centre at Phillip's former house in Bennett Street, Bath, but they had to be abandoned in 1989. The memorial tablet in the Abbey has a bronze relief portrait of the Admiral and is surmounted by the arms of the Commonwealth. It was unveiled by Viscount Wakefield in 1937.

BATHAMPTON WEIR.

137. This picture shows the weir at Bathampton around 1912. There were once mills on both sides on the weir, mainly for corn grinding. When water power lost its importance, the mill building became the popular Weir Tea Gardens. In 1966 Bath entrepreneur Keith Johnson opened it as the Keel Club. Later there was the Scanda Restaurant and finally another restaurant. It is now one of the Beefeater steak houses.

Bathford. N^r Bath. 1050

138. The ford across the Avon gave the village of Bathford its original name: Forde. The Crown Inn can be seen on the right; its mansard roof was changed in 1904. The house above it is Eagle House, known at Eaglehurst at that time. It became a school later and is now a hotel. Bathford Church and tower, completed in 1880, are on the right. Bath Electric Tramways Ltd., had not commenced their services to Bathford at the time when this picture was taken. From 1904 until 1939, trams ran between here and Combe Down every few minutes, from 5.30 a.m. till 11.40 p.m. on weekdays, and from 10.30 a.m. till 11 p.m. on Sundays.

Brown's Folly, Bathford.
From this Tower can be seen the Bristol Channel & Westbury White Horse.

139. Brown's Folly also known locally as the Pepperpot was built on Farleigh Down in 1848 by Mr. Wade Brown, a local landowner. In its early days it was used by the Ordnance Survey for their work, and during the First World War it served as an observation post: rambling was strictly forbidden in the vicinity. In 1972 Somerset Trust for Nature Conservation bought the folly and made the area around it into a nature reserve. In 1984 Avon Wildlife Trust extended the reserve by buying 63 more acres of woodlands. The Trust and Friends of the Earth, who now jointly manage it, had an ingenious fundraising idea in 1987: they sold one metre square plots of the reserve to the nature-loving public for £12, legal costs and full ownership rights included. In this way they hope to ensure that the area around Brown's Folly is protected from future development.

Monkton Combe, Canal Cottage.

140. The postcard's stamp is 1906, but the view may have been taken some years earlier. The Somerset Coal Canal connected the Kennet & Avon Canal with collieries in North Somerset. It was started in 1794 and a prosperous concern, until railway competition caused its gradual decline. In its heydays villagers would have seen many narrow boats drawn by horses or mules passing through Monkton Combe on the canal. It closed in 1898, and railway lines were built in replacement. At Monkton Combe this was the Camerton and Limpley Stoke Railway, now defunct as well. In many places only the line of the old canal embankment is visible today, but there has been much restoration, too. At Dundas Wharf a stretch of the SCC is now open again, for use as moorings.